STIONS OF AMERICAN HISTORY

WHO WROTE THE U.S. CONSTITUTION?

And Other Questions about the Constitutional Convention of 1787

Candice Ransom

LERNER PUBLICATIONS COMPANY · MINNEAPOLIS

A Word about Language

English word usage, spelling, grammar, and punctuation have changed over the centuries. We have preserved original spellings and word usage in the quotations included in this book.

Lerner Publications Company
A division of Lerner Publishing Group, Inc.
241 First Avenue North
Minneapolis, MN 55401 U.S.A.

Website address: www.lernerbooks.com

Library of Congress Cataloging-in-Publication Data

Ransom, Candice F., 1952–
    Who wrote the U.S. Constitution? And other questions about the Constitutional
Convention of 1787 / by Candice Ransom.
        p.   cm. — (Six questions of American history)
    Includes bibliographical references and index.
    ISBN 978–1–58013–669–3 (lib. bdg. : alk. paper)
    1. United States. Constitutional Convention (1787)—Juvenile literature.
2. United States. Constitution—Juvenile literature. 3. United States—Politics and
government—1783–1789—Juvenile literature. 4. Constitutional history—United
States—Juvenile literature. I. Title. II. Title: Who wrote the US Constitution?
E303.R36 2011
320.973—dc22   2009047425

Manufactured in the United States of America
1 – DP – 7/15/10

TABLE OF CONTENTS **4**

THE SIX QUESTIONS HELP YOU DISCOVER THE FACTS!

INTRODUCTION

On a May day in 1787, a stagecoach bounced over a rough Pennsylvania road. The coach's passenger had been riding for days through the countryside. The journey was uncomfortable, but the quiet passenger knew it was worth it. He had worked for months to prepare for a meeting in Philadelphia. In the distance, he spotted church spires of the city. Almost there!

Ten days later, a tall, broad-shouldered man arrived at the outskirts of Philadelphia. He came to the city to attend the same important meeting. The man was a famous army general. City officials honored him with a thirteen-gun salute— one cannon for each of the thirteen states.

Those states were originally thirteen colonies, ruled by Great Britain. In 1776 the colonies declared their independence. They wanted to be free of British rule. The quiet man and the tall man helped lead the country through a war against Britain. In 1781 the colonies won their freedom. They became the United States of America. The new nation adopted the Articles of Confederation—a set of rules for the U.S. government. Leaders thought the Articles of Confederation were the right plan for the country. But over the course of the 1780s, it became clear that the plan was not working. The country was in trouble. Unless something was done, the United States might break apart. In 1786 state representatives began planning a meeting to discuss how to fix the Articles of Confederation.

PACIFIC

OCEAN

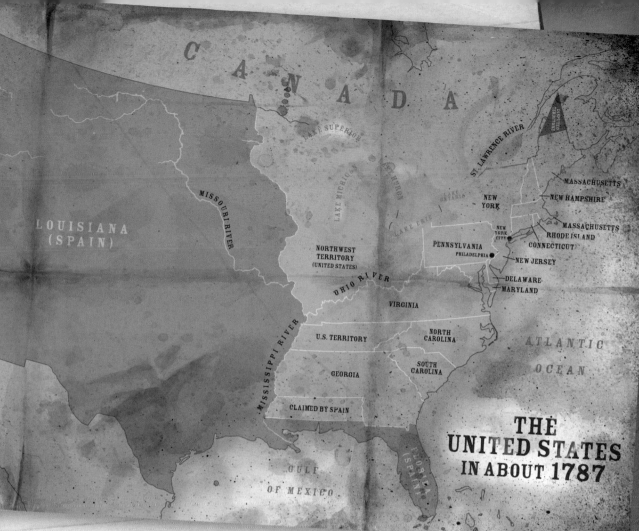

CANADA

LOUISIANA
(SPAIN)

MISSOURI RIVER

LAKE SUPERIOR

LAKE MICHIGAN

LAKE HURON

LAKE ONTARIO

LAKE ERIE

ST. LAWRENCE RIVER

MASSACHUSETTS

NEW HAMPSHIRE

NEW
YORK

MASSACHUSETTS

NEW
YORK
CITY

RHODE ISLAND

CONNECTICUT

PENNSYLVANIA

PHILADELPHIA

NEW JERSEY

DELAWARE

MARYLAND

NORTHWEST
TERRITORY
(UNITED STATES)

OHIO RIVER

VIRGINIA

U.S. TERRITORY

NORTH
CAROLINA

MISSISSIPPI RIVER

GEORGIA

SOUTH
CAROLINA

ATLANTIC

OCEAN

CLAIMED BY SPAIN

GULF

OF MEXICO

FLORIDA
(SPAIN)

THE
UNITED STATES
IN ABOUT 1787

Soon after arriving in Philadelphia, the tall man stopped at a brick house on a quiet street. He was shown in and greeted by an elderly man wearing glasses. The man's simple clothes did not show that he was famous around the world. The two men talked about the meeting, which was due to start the following day. Others were making their way to the city too. Most believed they were meeting to fix the Articles of Confederation. But these three had different ideas. Who were these three men?

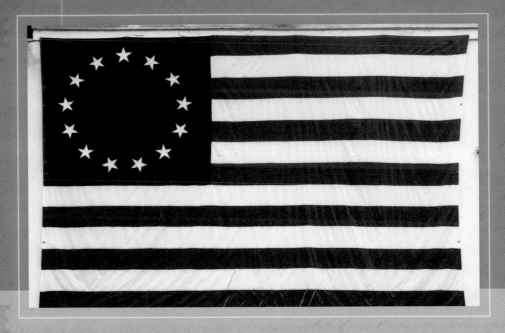

This flag, made by American Betsy Ross, has thirteen stars and thirteen stripes. The stars and stripes represented each of the original thirteen colonies.

ONE GATHERING

from 1775 to 1783, a conflict between Great Britain and its American colonies. The British surrendered in 1781. The war officially ended in 1783 with the Treaty of Paris.

The three men who gathered—James Madison, George Washington, and Benjamin Franklin—helped lead the colonies during the Revolutionary War. Like many American colonists, they had thought British rule was unfair. They felt that Great Britain had given the colonists no control over how they were governed.

After the revolution, the Articles of Confederation loosely held together the thirteen U.S. states. But most citizens were more loyal to their states than to the new nation. They called themselves New Yorkers or

Pennsylvanians rather than Americans. They did not think of the states as working together under one nation.

Many people were also suspicious of a strong federal government. They had just overthrown a large, controlling government. Why would they want another? So the articles allowed each state to run its own government. Each state had its own laws and its own way of doing business with other states.

federal: a central or national power that unites a group of states

Under the articles, state governments were stronger than the federal government. The federal government could not force states to pay taxes to support the country. It could not control how states dealt with one another or even with foreign countries.

> **"'Tis a universal [feeling] that our present system is a bad one. . . . A convention would revive the hopes of the people."**
>
> —Alexander Hamilton, a New York delegate to the 1787 convention

Alexander Hamilton

The federal government also had no leader, such as a president. It was not guided by a group of lawmakers elected by the people. The country had only the Confederation Congress, made up of delegates sent by each state. These problems and others faced the delegates as they gathered for the federal convention in Philadelphia.

On Monday, May 14, 1787, Madison left Mrs. Mary House's boardinghouse, where he was staying. He walked briskly through a light rain.

At 5 feet 4 inches (1.6 meters) and barely 100 (45 kilograms) pounds, James Madison wasn't a man people noticed. He was shy and spoke with a soft voice. But he carried big, bold ideas in his head. Madison was only thirty-six years old. Yet he had already served three terms in the Confederation Congress. In 1787 he was serving as a lawmaker in Virginia's state government.

James Madison was one of seven delegates sent to the convention by the state of Virginia.

8

On his walk through Philadelphia, Madison met up with Washington. They walked together, heading for the same place.

People gawked at Washington as he strode down the street. More than 6 feet (1.8 m) tall, he towered over most men of the day. His hands and feet were unusually large. But it wasn't just his size that made people stare. Washington was the most important man in the United States.

During the Revolutionary War, Washington had commanded the Continental Army, the colonial fighting force. After eight years of war, Washington led his troops to victory. He left the army in 1783, but everyone still called him General.

Washington had not wanted to leave his home in Virginia to go to the convention. When Madison first asked him to attend, Washington said no. But Washington, like Madison and other delegates, knew the Articles of Confederation were not working. If Washington could help save the United States in any way, he would do it. He decided to go to Philadelphia.

Madison and Washington reached the Pennsylvania State House (later renamed Independence Hall). Inside, Madison noted that only a small number of delegates were present. Seventy-four men had been invited. Fifty-five came. Every state except Rhode Island sent delegates. But on that Monday morning, only a few from Virginia and Pennsylvania gathered in the East Room. Of the Pennsylvanians, Benjamin Franklin was absent.

Franklin was eighty-one years old and in poor health. Yet his presence at the meeting was needed. The delegates—like most Americans— greatly respected Franklin. He was one of the signers of the Declaration of Independence. He was a writer, an

General George Washington was famous throughout the new United States for his role in gaining victory against the British in the Revolutionary War.

THE FRAMERS

Madison, Washington, and Franklin were three of the fifty-five delegates representing the people of their states. All delegates were chosen by their state governments. They were all white males. Most were wealthy. Twenty-nine had fought in the Revolutionary War. Eight had signed the Declaration of Independence. Many had served or were serving in the U.S. government. We call these people the Framers because they framed, or created, rules to govern the new nation.

inventor, a diplomat, and a political leader.

someone who works with foreign governments

Madison was disappointed with the convention turnout so far. But he realized that travel was uncertain. Some of the delegates lived only blocks away. But others had to travel up to 800 miles (1,287 kilometers). They traveled on horseback or by stagecoach or carriage. A single rainstorm could wash out roads and delay travelers. Without the rest of the delegates—and Dr. Franklin—the convention was not getting off to a good start.

NEXT QUESTION

WHO WAS VOTED PRESIDENT OF THE CONVENTION?

This painting by Jean Leon Gerome Ferris (1863–1930) shows Benjamin Franklin *(center right)* arriving at the State House in May 1787.

TWO THE CONVENTION BEGINS

By Friday, May 25, 1787, twenty-nine delegates had arrived in the city. That was enough to officially begin the convention. The delegates walked through rain-soaked streets to the State House. Philadelphia was a good place to hold the convention. With forty thousand people, it was the largest city in the nation. Museums, libraries, and public gardens were tucked between tidy two-story brick houses.

At the State House, delegates filed into the East Room on the first floor. Tall, wide windows along two walls provided light. The room was large, but not so large that members had to shout to be heard.

Thirteen tables—one for each state—formed a semicircle. The tables were covered in green cloths. They all faced a high-backed chair on a raised platform. A half sun was carved into the top of the chair.

Two or three armchairs were grouped around each table. The delegates from the northern states sat on one end of the semicircle. Southern delegates sat on the opposite end. Delegates from the central states sat in the middle.

The delegates voted Washington president of the convention. He sat on the high-backed chair on the platform. James Madison chose a seat front and center. He would sit in this chair every day, his pen scratching as he took detailed notes of each speech and debate.

The delegates elected a young law student, William Jackson, as the convention's secretary. It was Jackson's job to record the convention's voting results.

WHERE IS INDEPENDENCE HALL?
Independence Hall is in downtown Philadelphia, on Chestnut Street between 6th Street and 5th Street. Since 1951 the building has been part of the Independence National Historic Park.

debate: a discussion among people with different opinions. At meetings such as the convention, an issue is debated to help delegates decide how to vote.

13

That first day, the delegates also formed a rules committee. The committee created rules for discussing and voting on convention issues. Each state—no matter how large or small—got one vote.

Nine more delegates arrived over the weekend of May 26 and May 27. On Monday, May 28, Franklin attended for the first time. Walking or riding in a carriage was too painful for Franklin. So he was carried into the East Room on a special chair called a sedan chair.

This modern photograph shows the East Room, or Assembly Room, of the State House (Independence Hall). The National Park Service restored the room in 1956 to make it look as it did in 1787.

John Trumball's 1817 painting *The Declaration of Independence (above),* shows the leaders of the early U.S. government working in the East Room of the Pennsylvania State House.

At ten o'clock, the rules committee started the meeting. Under the rules, speakers addressed the convention president, not the other delegates. A member could speak once but not again until the others had a chance to make their first speech. A vote would be won by the majority of states present.

Five convention delegates stayed at the Indian Queen Tavern (above, center). Many delegates also met at the tavern each evening for group dinners.

WHERE DID THEY STAY?

Delegates from other states had to find someplace to stay while in Philadelphia. Some stayed with friends. Others paid for rooms at places such as the Indian Queen Tavern, the City Tavern, and Mrs. Marshall's boardinghouse. A tavern was an inn, somewhat like a modern hotel. A boardinghouse is a home in which the owner rents rooms.

Delegates could postpone a vote and bring back issues for discussion as often as needed.

A rule of secrecy was added the next day. All convention votes, speeches, debates, and notes were to be kept strictly private. No one could give comments to newspapers or discuss meeting business with anyone outside the convention. The spring weather was very warm in Philadelphia. But the East Room's windows remained closed. Guards were posted outside the door. With this rule, delegates felt free to bring up ideas without worrying what the public thought. The delegates were ready to begin the real business of the convention.

WHO WAS *NOT* AT THE CONVENTION?

Some famous U.S. patriots were missing from the convention. Political leaders Thomas Jefferson and John Adams were in Europe working as diplomats. Revolutionary War leader Patrick Henry was invited to the convention. But he said he "smelt a rat" and refused to attend. Samuel Adams, also a leader in the revolution, stayed home too. Neither Henry nor Samuel Adams wanted huge changes to the Articles of Confederation. They did not want a federal government with greater control over the states or over citizens.

NEXT QUESTION

WHO SPOKE FIRST?

This 1781 Virginia banknote was used as money. The U.S. government did not make dollars and coins until the 1790s.

THREE A NEW PLAN

Virginia governor Edmund Randolph spoke first on Tuesday, May 29, 1787. Randolph brought up the problems with the Articles of Confederation. Many states argued over borders shared with other states. People had trouble conducting business across state lines. State governments had no money. Some states printed money. But the money was not backed up by gold or silver. Much of it was worthless.

Randolph spoke about another serious problem—taxes. The cost of the Revolutionary War left the United States in debt. The government owed money to wealthy U.S. citizens and to foreign countries such as France and

owing money

NEW
HAMPSHIRE

MASSACHUSETTS

BOSTON

RHODE
ISLAND

CONNECTICUT

NEW
YORK

NEW
JERSEY

PENNSYLVANIA

DELAWARE

MARYLAND

BRITISH

TERRITORY

VIRGINIA

This map shows the
original American
colonies that were
ruled by Great Britain.
After the Revolutionary
War, the colonies
became U.S. states.

NORTH
CAROLINA

ATLANTIC
OCEAN

SOUTH
CAROLINA

GEORGIA

THE ORIGINAL
THIRTEEN
COLONIES

GULF
OF
MEXICO

the Netherlands. To raise money to pay the debt, the U.S.
government asked each state to tax its residents.

Not every state agreed to do so. But states such as Virginia
and Massachusetts taxed their citizens. Taxes had to be paid
in cash. And that was a problem for many people. Ordinary
working people did not use much cash. They lived off what
they owned and grew—their land, houses, tools, livestock,
and crops. If they needed something—a new tool or a pair of
boots—they traded for it. But they could not trade with the
state to pay their taxes.

This needlepoint by Mary Woodhull (1743–1815) shows a New England harvest scene. For most people, farming was a way of producing food and supplies rather than making money.

The situation was especially bad for farmers. States began taking to court farmers who could not pay their taxes and other debts. The courts took away farmers' land and livestock. Some farmers were even thrown in prison.

During the summer of 1786, hundreds of angry Massachusetts farmers formed a rebel force. One of the leaders was Daniel Shays, a Revolutionary War hero, politician, and farmer. From August 1786 to January 1787, the rebels stormed courthouses in Northhampton, Worcester, and other Massachusetts towns.

rebel someone who fights against an authority, such as a government

This woodcut shows Daniel Shays (*left*) and fellow rebel leader Job Shattuck. The image was printed in *Bickerstaff's Boston Almanack* in 1787.

WHY WAS SHAYS'S REBELLION IMPORTANT?

In October 1786, the Confederation Congress decided to use federal troops to stop the rebels. But Congress could not convince state governments to help pay for the soldiers. Massachusetts leaders had to raise the money themselves. In January 1787, Shays and his rebels attacked an armory (a building used to store weapons) in Springfield, Massachusetts. Troops stopped the raid, and many rebels were arrested.

In the spring of 1787, Massachusetts passed laws to help farmers in debt. The rebellion began to fade. But for many people, Shays's Rebellion showed how weak the federal government was. For them, it proved that the Articles of Confederation were failing.

They forced the courts to close. Shays's Rebellion shocked the country.

With all these problems before them, what could the convention delegates do?

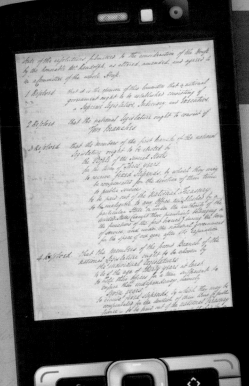

Randolph presented a plan written by James Madison and other Virginia delegates. The Virginia Plan created a stronger federal government— one that could protect the American people.

Randolph explained that the plan created a national legislature. The legislature had two branches. Members of the first branch (the House of Representatives) would be elected by the people. House members would choose delegates to the second branch (the Senate). Together, the House and Senate would elect the U.S. president and federal judges.

legislature: an organized group of people with the power to make laws

Edmund Randolph

Randolph spoke for more than three hours. At last, he sat down. The first real meeting of the convention had left the delegates with much to think about.

The next day, May 30, forty-one delegates began going over the Virginia Plan point by point. The Articles of Confederation had set up the Confederation Congress as the federal government. But the articles also protected each state's freedom and independence. Under the Virginia Plan, the federal government could overrule state governments. Delegates realized that the Virginia Plan did not correct the Articles. It ignored them altogether.

This idea stopped several delegates in their tracks. They thought they were at the convention to revise and strengthen the Articles of Confederation. They did *not* expect a new plan that threw out the Articles. Did they dare change the entire system of government?

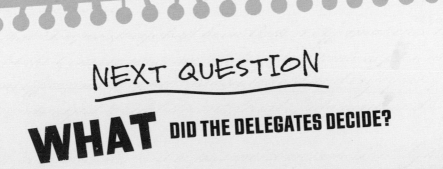

NEXT QUESTION

WHAT DID THE DELEGATES DECIDE?

The sun chair used by George Washington stands in the East Room of Independence Hall. The chair is the only piece of original furniture in the restored room.

FOUR SEPARATION OF POWERS

On May 31, 1787, convention delegates voted to create a stronger national government. They decided that it should consist of three parts: the legislative, the executive, and the judicial. The legislative part, called Congress, would make the laws. The president would be the head of the executive part. He would carry out the laws. The national court system was the judicial part. It would decide the meaning of the laws and if they were being obeyed. With three parts, or branches, power would be shared. No one branch would have more control of the federal government than the other two.

judicial – relating to courts and judges

Discussion swung to the one-vote-for-one-state system described in the Articles of Confederation. In 1787 a state's importance was measured by the number of its citizens. For example, Georgia had a lot of land. But it was still considered small because of its low population. The three biggest states—Virginia, Pennsylvania, and Massachusetts—held nearly half the nation's population. But under the articles, each state had only one vote, no matter its size or population. Tiny Rhode Island's voice in Congress carried as much weight as mighty Massachusetts. This is called equal representation.

the number of people living in an area such as a state or country

having someone act or speak for someone else

The Virginia Plan changed that. Under the plan, the House of Representatives would be elected by the people. And the number of representatives would be based on a state's population. The number of members in the Senate would also depend on population. This is known as proportional (an amount determined by size) representation.

"We ought to attend to the rights of every class of the people."

—Virginia delegate George Mason, arguing that the House of Representatives should be elected by the people

George Mason

Immediately, the convention broke into two camps: big states versus small states. The small states fought against the Virginia Plan. With proportional representation, they felt they would not have as strong a voice in the federal government.

The states had other differences beyond size. Southerners grew tobacco, sugar, and rice on large farms called plantations. Many people in the middle of the country—Pennsylvania, New Jersey, Delaware, and New York—were merchants. They ran businesses and stores. People in Massachusetts and Connecticut were shipbuilders and fishers.

Slavery was another big issue dividing the states. Southern plantation owners used African slaves to work the plantations. Slaves were treated as property. Slavery was against the law in most northern states. Some northerners wanted to make slavery illegal in every state. But southern states fiercely defended their right to own slaves.

Slavery holding other people as property, forcing them to work without pay, and denying them basic freedoms

This hand-colored print shows African slaves working in the field at Mount Vernon. Mount Vernon was George Washington's plantation in Virginia.

At the 1787 convention, slavery became part of the debate over proportional representation. Should slaves be counted as part of a state's population? Thousands of slaves lived in states such as Georgia and South Carolina. Counting slaves would give southern states more representatives in the federal government. Northern delegates felt this was unfair. Southern states did not treat slaves like people in any other case. Why should they be allowed to use the slave population to gain more representation?

Day after day, the delegates chewed over parts of the representation issue. The room grew hot. The hours grew long.

The Virginians had taken control of the convention. Their delegates were good writers and speakers.

But Virginia was not the entire nation. The small states needed to be heard. William Paterson, a New Jersey lawyer, presented the New Jersey Plan. It was the small states' answer to the Virginia Plan.

William Paterson

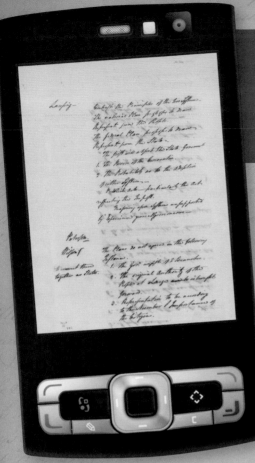

William Paterson made these notes *(left)* while preparing to defend his New Jersey Plan at the convention. His handwritten notes are part of the Manuscript Division of the Library of Congress in Washington, D.C.

Under the New Jersey Plan, Congress would have only one house. It would not have a House of Representatives and a Senate. The federal government would not have a president. And there would be no federal courts except the Supreme Court.

The New Jersey Plan proposed that all states—no matter how big or small—would have the same number of representatives. Most important, Paterson's plan did not create a new constitution. The plan was designed to become additional amendments, or formal changes, to the Articles of Confederation.

On June 19, James Madison jumped to his feet to speak first. He wanted to convince the delegates to vote for the Virginia Plan. He argued against the New Jersey Plan point by point. When he was finished, the delegates voted.

Seven states chose the Virginia Plan. Three states voted for the New Jersey Plan. (Maryland was divided and did not cast a vote). The big states had won. For the next several days, members argued. Two houses in Congress or one? The same issues were brought up but never solved. Tempers flared. The small states felt the big states were pushing them around again.

JAMES MADISON

James Madison was a key player at the convention even before the meeting began. He had read about the governments of modern and ancient civilizations. From his studies, he came up with two theories. The first was that a national government should come from the people and not the states. The second was that powers should be divided so no one person or group controlled the government.

While waiting for the rest of the members to arrive, the Virginia delegates met each morning at Mrs. House's boardinghouse. Using James Madison's theories, the group hammered out the Virginia Plan.

NEXT QUESTION

HOW DID THE DELEGATES BEGIN WORKING TOGETHER?

FIVE THE GREAT COMPROMISE

July 2, 1787, was a Monday. By the time the delegates met in the morning, the East Room was already hot. Once again, delegates voted on whether states should have equal representation in the Senate. Five states said yes, five said no, and Georgia was divided. A tie. Everyone was discouraged.

Benjamin Franklin understood that each state had to give up something in order for everyone to gain. He suggested a compromise. The delegates could choose parts from the Virginia and New Jersey plans that would please both the big and small states.

an agreement to give up some demands in order to get others

A GOOD COMPROMISER

Benjamin Franklin urged delegates to settle convention issues by compromise. He often hosted dinner parties to make the delegates feel more at home in Philadelphia. The parties also gave the delegates a chance to get to know one another better. That made it easier for delegates to discuss and decide issues at the convention.

The delegates took off the next two days for Independence Day. On July 4, bells rang and guns fired salutes. People celebrated the country's freedom from British rule. Few knew that the entire convention was on the brink of failure.

When the members met again on July 5, they took up the same argument.

These life-size bronze statues of convention delegates are at the National Constitution Center in Philadelphia. Benjamin Franklin is shown seated, holding a cane.

WHAT ABOUT SLAVERY?

Should slaves be counted as part of a southern state's population? To solve that debate, northern and southern delegates reached another compromise. They agreed that a slave would count as three-fifths of a free person. In other words, for every five slaves living in a state, three were counted for the purpose of proportional representation and taxes. This became known as the Three-Fifths Compromise, or the Three-Fifths Clause.

Then Connecticut's Roger Sherman came up with a solution. He pointed out that the big states had already won proportional representation in the lower house. He proposed that each state, no matter what size, would send two delegates to the upper house.

The members debated Sherman's proposal for eleven days.

"In the second branch or Senate, each state should have one vote and no more. . . . As the states would remain possessed of certain individual rights, each state ought to be able to protect itself."

—Connecticut delegate Roger Sherman

Roger Sherman

On July 16, they
voted again.
The Connecticut
Compromise passed,
five votes to four.
This vote, also
known as the Great
Compromise, became
a turning point in the
convention. Delegates from
big states and small realized that
they needed to think about the greater good of the nation.
Almost as a sign that the right decision had been made,
Philadelphia's heat wave broke.

Next, the delegates wrestled with the question of the
president. How long should he serve? Eleven years? Fifteen?
Should the president be appointed by Congress or elected
by the people? James Wilson brought up the idea of
electors. Electors were people chosen by the state to vote in
a presidential election. But the members didn't like Wilson's
scheme.

Convention members voted over and over. They sometimes voted again on issues they had already settled. Through it all, George Washington sat in the high-backed chair and listened. Most members believed that Washington would be the perfect first president. He had already proved to be a strong leader. And people liked him. But who would be president after Washington? The delegates knew they had to be careful about the way future presidents would be elected.

On July 26, the convention took a ten-day break. Delegates who lived close by went home. Others headed for cooler air in the mountains. Washington visited Valley Forge, a rural area northwest of Philadelphia. During the Revolutionary War, Washington and his troops had camped at Valley Forge. Freezing and hungry, they spent the winter of 1777 and 1778 in tiny log huts. The old camp was in ruins when Washington visited it that July.

Washington (right) and an army officer walk past troops at Valley Forge during the winter of 1777 and 1778. This image is a print made of a painting by Howard Pyle (1853–1911).

Not everyone went on vacation. Five delegates remained in Philadelphia. John Rutledge, Nathaniel Gorham, Oliver Ellsworth, Edmund Randolph, and James Wilson made up the Committee of Detail. They had the important job of copying down the resolutions that had been decided so far. It was hard work. But they finished a rough outline of a document. The document was a new plan for the government—a constitution. The draft was printed and ready to be handed out when the convention met again.

NEXT QUESTION

WHAT HAPPENED TO THE DOCUMENT?

This is a copy of the U.S. Constitution. The original U.S. Constitution is kept in the National Archives Building in Washington, D.C.

SIX OF AND FOR THE PEOPLE

On Monday, August 6, delegates received their copies of the Constitution—seven freshly inked pages. Starting the next day and all through hot, steamy August, they debated every sentence.

The Constitution had twenty-three articles. Each article was divided into sections. The delegates needed to speed up the process of discussing and voting on all the articles. To achieve this, many items were given to committees to settle.

The Committee of Postponed Parts had the most issues to work out. It had to decide where the new government would be located and how Congress would charge taxes.

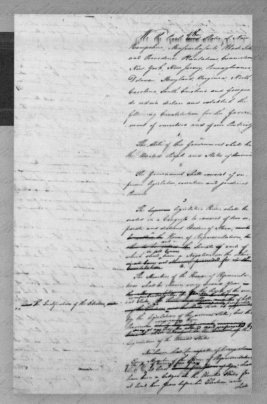

But the executive branch was its most pressing problem.

The Committee of Postponed Parts decided the president of the United States would serve a term of four years and could be reelected. He must be a U.S. citizen and at least thirty-five years old.

The committee added the office of vice president. The vice president would lead the Senate and take over if the president died or had to leave office. The members made sure the president and Congress had the power to get things done. But each branch would not have too much power over the other.

A huge question remained. How would the country choose the president? Most delegates felt the president should be selected by Congress or state legislatures. Back in June, James Wilson said the people should pick the president. No one had liked that idea. But members of the committee changed their minds. They agreed that Wilson's plan was a good one after all.

Wilson's plan included what came to be called the electoral college. The country would be divided into areas, or districts. People from each district would choose an elector. Those electors would decide who would be president.

The Committee of Style revised the final draft of the Constitution. Gouverneur Morris wrote the preamble

with its stirring words: "*We, the People of the United States. . . .*" The U.S. Constitution became a document of and for the people.

The final version was presented to the convention on September 12. George Mason felt that there should be a Bill of Rights—a list of important rights guaranteed to citizens. Elbridge Gerry agreed, but the other members did not. They believed people's rights were already protected by state constitutions.

Gouverneur Morris (left) was a convention delegate from Pennsylvania. This engraving of Morris was made from an original painting by Ezra Ames (1768–1836).

On Monday, September 17, forty-two delegates were present. William Jackson, the convention secretary, read aloud the final version of the Constitution. Benjamin Franklin gave a speech to James Wilson to read for him. Franklin did not like parts of the Constitution. But even with its faults, he doubted anyone could create a better system of government. He urged each man present to sign the Constitution.

George Washington signed first. Then state by state, thirty-nine delegates signed their names. Secretary Jackson witnessed their signatures. Three men refused to sign. Edmund Randolph, George Mason, and Elbridge Gerry would not sign without a Bill of Rights.

Convention delegates used this silver pen and ink set to sign the U.S. Constitution on September 17, 1787. The set is on display in the East Room of Independence Hall.

Delegates celebrated the end of the convention at City Tavern *(left)* on Second Street in Philadelphia. Built in 1773, the tavern remains a popular restaurant and tourist spot.

When the Constitution was signed, Franklin pointed to the half sun carved on the back of Washington's chair. He said he never could tell if the sun was rising or setting. But now he knew that it was a rising sun. That evening the delegates held a farewell dinner at the City Tavern. They had come to Philadelphia with different ideas and interests. During the summer, they learned to work together. The result was the U.S. Constitution.

The Constitution was written and signed. But it still had to be ratified, or approved, by nine out of thirteen states. Over the next few months, citizens in every state learned how the Constitution would work. James Madison and others wrote essays to explain the document. Delaware was the first state to ratify it—on December 7, 1787. When the ninth state, New Hampshire, ratified it on June 21, 1788, the Constitution became law.

WHAT IS THE BILL OF RIGHTS?

The Framers of the Constitution believed that every person had specific rights that could not be taken away by any government. Some Framers thought those rights should be written down in the Constitution. Others felt it was impossible to list all the rights of a citizen. But as they worked to get the Constitution ratified, the Framers discovered that people were worried. Was the new U.S. government too powerful? Would it use its power against citizens? Maybe the Constitution needed a bill of rights, after all.

The Bill of Rights was written by James Madison in 1789 as a series of articles. The articles were voted on by the states. On December 15, 1791, the Bill of Rights became part of the U.S. Constitution.

The story was not yet over. The Bill of Rights would be added in 1791. The Bill of Rights is made up of the first ten constitutional amendments. The Constitution would be amended seventeen more times between 1795 and 1992. The original Constitution and its amendments have guided the United States for more than two hundred years.

NEXT QUESTION

HOW DO WE KNOW WHAT HAPPENED AT THE CONSTITUTIONAL CONVENTION?

Primary Source: James Madison's Notes

The best way to see into the past and learn about any historical event is with primary sources. Primary sources are created near the time being studied. They include diaries, letters, newspaper articles, documents, speeches, personal papers, pamphlets, photos, paintings, and other items. They are made by people who have direct, firsthand knowledge of the event.

None of the Constitutional Convention delegates talked to newspaper reporters or other outsiders. Some delegates took notes, but not every day. Even secretary William Jackson's records were incomplete. So how do we know what went on behind those closed doors?

James Madison gave us our only complete primary source. Every day, he sat at the front of the East Room and recorded the day's events. After the Convention, he wrote about his task:

> I noted in terms legible [readable] and in abbreviations and marks intelligible [understandable] to myself what was read [by George Washington] or spoken by the members; and . . . I was enabled to write out my daily notes during the session or within a few finishing days after its close. . . . I was not absent a single day, nor more than a . . . fraction of an hour in any day, so that I could not have lost a single speech, unless a very short one.

In the 1830s, Madison explained his reasons for keeping the daily convention accounts. He understood, he said, "the value of such a contribution to the fund of materials for the History of a Constitution on which would be staked the happiness of a people great even in its infancy, and possibly the cause of Liberty throughout the world."

Madison's Notes of the Debates in the Federal Convention are six hundred typed pages. For the most part, historians believe that his record of that important summer is honest and accurate.

TELL YOUR CONSTITUTIONAL CONVENTION STORY

Imagine you are a delegate from one of the twelve states represented at the Constitutional Convention in the summer of 1787. (Remember, Rhode Island chose not to send any delegates.) You keep a daily diary. Write several entries about your experience as a delegate.

WHERE are you from?

WHAT do you do for a living?

WHAT issues are most important to you?

HOW did you travel to Philadelphia?

WHAT do you hope happens at the convention?

WHO among the convention's leaders do you most admire? Why?

USE **WHO, WHAT, WHERE WHY, WHEN,** AND **HOW** TO THINK OF OTHER QUESTIONS TO HELP YOU CREATE YOUR STORY!

Timeline

1775
The Revolutionary War between the American colonies and Great Britain begins.

1776
On July 4, the Confederation Congress adopts the **Declaration of Independence.**

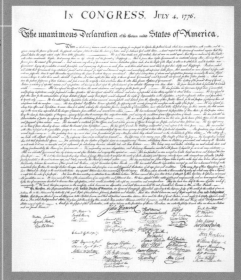

1777
The Confederation Congress adopts the Articles of Confederation.

1781
The British army surrenders at the last big battle of the Revolutionary War.

1783
The Revolutionary War ends when the United States and Great Britain sign the Treaty of Paris.

1786
State delegates begin planning a federal convention to discuss the Articles of Confederation.

1787
In January angry farmers attack the Springfield (Massachusetts) Armory during **Shays's Rebellion**.

In May delegates gather in Philadelphia for the federal convention.

On May 29, Edmund Randolph presents the Virginia Plan. William Paterson presents the New Jersey Plan on June 15.

In July, convention delegates agree to the Great Compromise. The Committee of Detail begins preparing a draft of the **U.S. Constitution**.

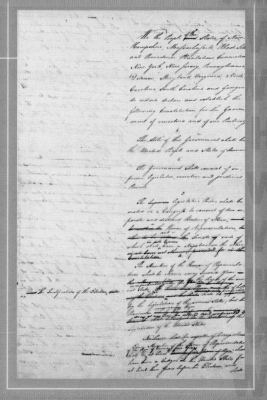

In September convention delegates reject George Mason and Elbridge Gerry's suggestion for a bill of rights. The convention adopts the Constitution.

In December Delaware becomes the first state to ratify the Constitution.

1788
In June New Hampshire becomes the ninth state to ratify it. The Constitution is signed into law.

1789
George Washington is unanimously chosen as first president of the United States.

1791
The Constitution is amended to include the Bill of Rights.

1793
George Washington is unanimously elected for a second term as U.S. president.

1956
The East Room of Independence Hall was restored to look as it did in 1787.

Source Notes

7 Alexander Hamilton, letter to James Duane, September 3, 1780, quoted in Richard Haesly, *The Constitutional Convention* (San Diego: Greenhaven, 2002), 51.

25 Catherine Drinker Bowen, *Miracle at Philadelphia: The Story of the Constitutional Convention May to September 1787* (Boston: Little Brown, 1966), 47.

32 Roger Sherman, quoted in Richard Beeman, *Plain, Honest Men: The Making of the American Constitution* (New York: Random House, 2009), 150.

42 Merrill D. Peterson, ed., *James Madison: A Biography in His Own Words,* vol. I (New York: Newsweek, 1974), 131.

42 ibid.

Selected Bibliography

Beeman, Richard. *Plain, Honest Men: The Making of the American Constitution.* New York: Random House, 2009.

Bowen, Catherine Drinker. *Miracle at Philadelphia: The Story of the Constitutional Convention May to September 1787.* Boston: Little Brown, 1966.

Collier, Christopher, and James Lincoln Collier. *Decision in Philadelphia: The Constitution Convention of 1787.* New York: Random House, 1986.

Haesly, Richard, ed. *The Constitutional Convention.* San Diego: Greenhaven Press, 2002.

Hauptly, Denis J. *"A Convention of Delegates": The Creation of the Constitution.* New York: Atheneum, 1987.

Kurland, Philip B., and Ralph Lerner, eds. *The Founders' Constitution.* 2000. http://press-pubs.uchicago.edu/founders (April 23, 2010).

LeVert, Suzanne. *The Constitution.* New York: Marshall Cavendish, 2003.

Peterson, Merrill D., ed. *James Madison: A Biography in His Own Words.* Vol. I. New York: Newsweek, 1974.

Stewart, David O. *The Summer of 1787: The Men Who Invented the Constitution.* New York: Simon and Schuster, 2007.

Willis, Garry. *James Madison.* New York: Holt, 2002.

Further Reading and Websites

Catrow, David. *We the Kids: The Preamble to the Constitution of the United States*. New York: Dial, 2002. Illustrated with cartoons, this fun book tells the story of how three kids and a dog explore the meaning of the Preamble to the Constitution.

Cheney, Lynne. *We the People: The Story of Our Constitution*. New York: Simon and Schuster, 2008. With lively illustrations, this book covers the events from the end of the Revolutionary War through the Constitutional Convention.

The Constitution for Kids
http://www.usconstitution.net/constkids4.html
This site includes pictures of the U.S. Constitution, the history of the document, and information on issues such as slavery and states' rights.

Constitution: Travel Back in History
http://www.congressforkids.net/Constitution_delegates.htm
This site contains information about what happened at the convention and how the U.S. Constitution works. It also features questions to think about and a list of books to read.

Feldman, Ruth Tenzer. *How Congress Works*. Minneapolis: Lerner Publications Company, 2004. See how the modern U.S. Congress operates under the rules set down in the Constitution.

Mitchell, Barbara. *Father of the Constitution: A Story about James Madison*. Minneapolis: Millbrook Press, 2004. Mitchell offers an introduction to the life of James Madison, one of the Framers of the Constitution.

The National Constitutional Center: Founders
http://constitutioncenter.org/ncc_edu_Founders.aspx
Click on short biographies of each of the delegates who attended the convention. This site also contains a map of the thirteen states and surrounding territories.

Sherrow, Victoria. *Benjamin Franklin*. Minneapolis: Lerner Publications, 2002. Learn about Franklin's childhood, his inventions and writings, and how he helped shape the new United States of America.

Sobel, Syl. *The U.S. Constitution and You*. Hauppauge, New York: Barron's, 2001. This book tells how the Constitution works and how it protects the rights of every U.S. citizen, even kids!

Travis, Cathy. *Constitution Translated for Kids*. Austin, TX: Synergy Books: 2006. This book translates the Constitution sentence by sentence, with the original document in one column and the same text in simple language in a second column.

Index

Photo Acknowledgments

The images in this book are used with the permission of: National Archives, Constitution of the United States, backgrounds throughout book; © iStockphoto.com/DNY59, p. 1; © iStockphoto.com/sx70, pp. 3 (top), 7 (top), 11 (top), 15 (bottom), 16 (bottom), 17 (top), 21, (bottom), 29 (top), 31 (top), 32 (top), 41 (top); © iStockphoto.com/Ayse Nazli Deliormanli, p. 3 (bottom), 43 (left); © iStockphoto.com/Serdar Yagci (notebook background), pp. 4-5, 43; © Bill Hauser/Independent Picture Service, pp. 5, 9, 13 (inset), 19, 35 (inset); © Nikreates/Alamy, p. 6; © Stock Montage/Getty Images, p. 7 (bottom); Library of Congress, pp. 8 (LC-USZ62-16960), 22 (bottom, LC-D416-9861); © Huntington Library/SuperStock, p. 10; © SuperStock, pp. 12, 30; © iStockphoto.com/Talshiar (GPS), pp. 13, 35 (top); © Andre Jenny/Alamy, p. 14; © North Wind Picture Archives, p. 15 (top), 26; The Historical Society of Pennsylvania (HSP), Old Indian Queen Tavern – General View, (Bb 862 Ev15 51), p. 16 (top); The Granger Collection, New York, pp. 18, 20, 21 (top), 25, 36; © iStockphoto.com/Andrey Pustovoy (phone), pp. 22, 28, 39, 40; National Archives, pp. 22 (inset), 44 (top); © JJM Stock Photography/Travel/Alamy, p. 24; © Hulton Archive/Getty Images, pp. 27, 32, 38; Library of Congress, Manuscript Division (0059.01.00), p. 28 (inset); © age fotostock/SuperStock, p. 31 (bottom); © Smithsonian Art Museum, Washington, DC/Art Resource, NY, p. 33; © Pictorial Press/Alamy, p. 34; © Boltin Picture Library/The Bridgeman Art Library, pp. 37, 45; © J. McGrail/ClassicStock/The Image Works, p. 39 (inset); © Vespasian/Alamy, p. 40 (inset); © MPI/Stringer/Hulton Archive/Getty Images, p. 43 (right); © Art Resource, NY, p. 44 (bottom).

Front cover: © SuperStock.
Back cover background: National Archives, Constitution of the United States.